C000174922

Tor Mark

Published by Tor Mark
United Downs Industrial Estate,
St Day, Redruth, Cornwall TR16 5HY

www.tormark.co.uk

Published 2018

ISBN 978 0 85025 438 9

Printed by Booths Print,
The Praze, Penryn, Cornwall TR10 8AA

CORNISH RECIPES

Tamar Swift

CONTENTS

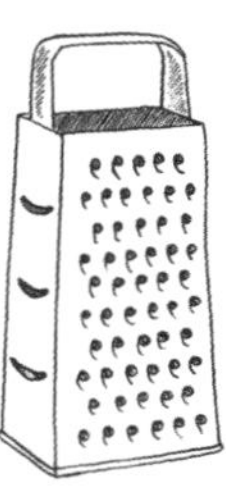

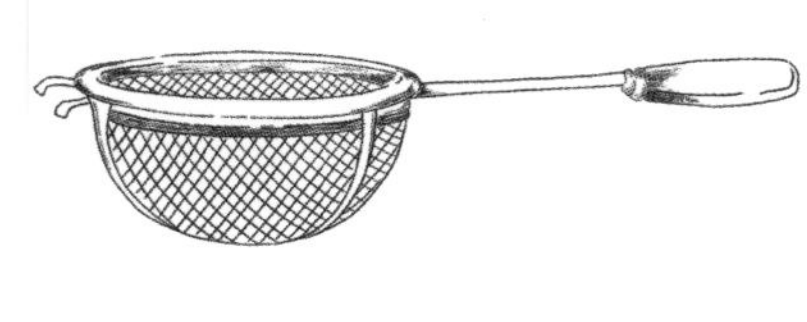

PROPER CORNISH PASTIES

A CORNISH CREAM TEA

CAKES & BAKES

SWEETS & TREATS

CORNISH COCKTAILS

FOR THE ADVENTUROUS...

AN INTRODUCTION

Cooking is now for everyone, with those eating having the final say in the 'proof of the pudding'. It is unlikely any visitor will leave Cornwall today without tasting its most delectable of treats, clotted cream. While this may have been the reserve of the 'fairer few' in the past, today's clotted cream is widely available throughout Cornwall in quantities and prices to suit everyone's pocket. While most think of this as a sweet addition, it is equally good stirred into curries and stroganoff, where its delicate hue gives a lighter and more subtle flavour than cheese.

For an extra-special treat, why not try one of Chapel Porth's Hedgehog Ice creams, with its topping of clotted cream finished off with 'dressings' of your design.

The Proper Cornish Pasty really has stood the test of time, being as it is, the original 'fast food'. While the traditional Cornish Pasty was made with potatoes, swede and a little meat, today's pasties vary according to the season and to taste. It is not uncommon to find a vast list of pasties on offer in a local bakery, including various forms of chicken, pork, rabbit, fish, eggs and vegetables. The recipes in this book reflect changes in Cornish pasty-making, so don't be afraid to get creative! Most ingredients work well in a pasty; the secret is to balance taste with texture, making sure you have an equal balance of the two.

Seasoning is a very good example of how cooking has changed over the centuries. In the past, this term generally referred to salt and pepper only. Today however this might include grated nutmeg, a pinch of cumin or, being Cornwall, a snaffle of Saffron. Again, experiment as you wish, choosing whichever spices suit your taste and those of your guests.

Whatever you cook, and whoever you do it for, enjoy!

Tamar Swift

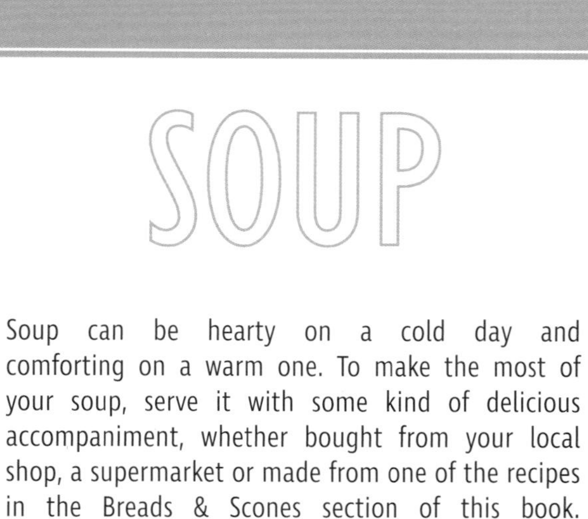

SOUP

Soup can be hearty on a cold day and comforting on a warm one. To make the most of your soup, serve it with some kind of delicious accompaniment, whether bought from your local shop, a supermarket or made from one of the recipes in the Breads & Scones section of this book.

FISH SOUP

225g haddock fillet or other white fish

1 medium onion, finely chopped

seasoning

740ml milk

50g butter

35g plain flour

chopped parsley

Place the fish in a saucepan with the onion, seasoning and milk. Simmer gently for 15 minutes or until the fish is cooked and flakes easily. Remove the fish from the milk and reserve the liquid.

Carefully flake the fish and set aside. Place the butter, flour and both the milk used to cook the fish and the extra 150ml into a pan and bring to a gentle simmer, stirring all the time.

Add the flaked fish and continue simmering until the fish is completely heated. Serve with a sprinkling of parsley.

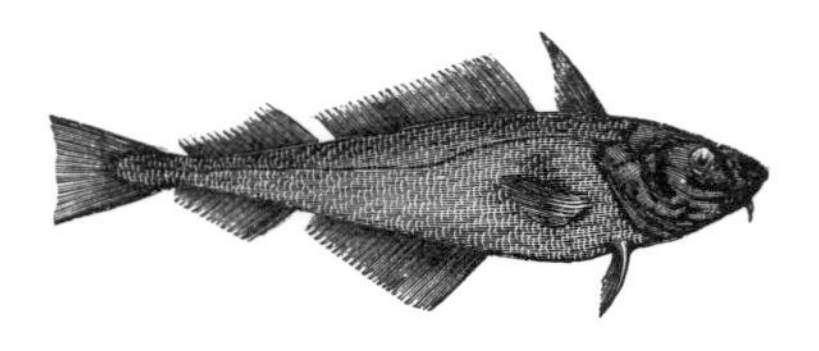

NETTLE SOUP

900g young nettles

560g spinach

720ml good stock

3 tbs plain flour

3 tbs sour/clotted cream

cold milk

4 sausages, cooked, cold and sliced into rounds

seasoning

Gather the tips of young stinging nettles, wearing gloves. Wash and blanch the nettles; wash and spin the spinach. Bring the stock to the boil before pouring it over both the nettles and spinach.

Season and simmer for 45 minutes, adding further water/stock if required. Pass the liquid through a sieve. Blend the flour, cream and milk to form a smooth paste.

Place all the ingredients (minus the cream/milk mixture), including the sliced sausages into a pan and bring to a gentle boil. Remove from the heat, stir in the cream mixture and serve.

LEEK & POTATO SOUP

1 rasher bacon

10g butter

2 large leeks

450g potatoes

360ml stock

salt and pepper

120ml milk

Chop the bacon into small pieces and fry lightly in a saucepan. Add the butter, sliced leeks and potatoes.

Cook over a gentle heat until the vegetables are tender. Add the stock, season well and cover. Simmer for a further 20 minutes.

Finally add the milk to the soup just before serving, re-heat and re-season if necessary.

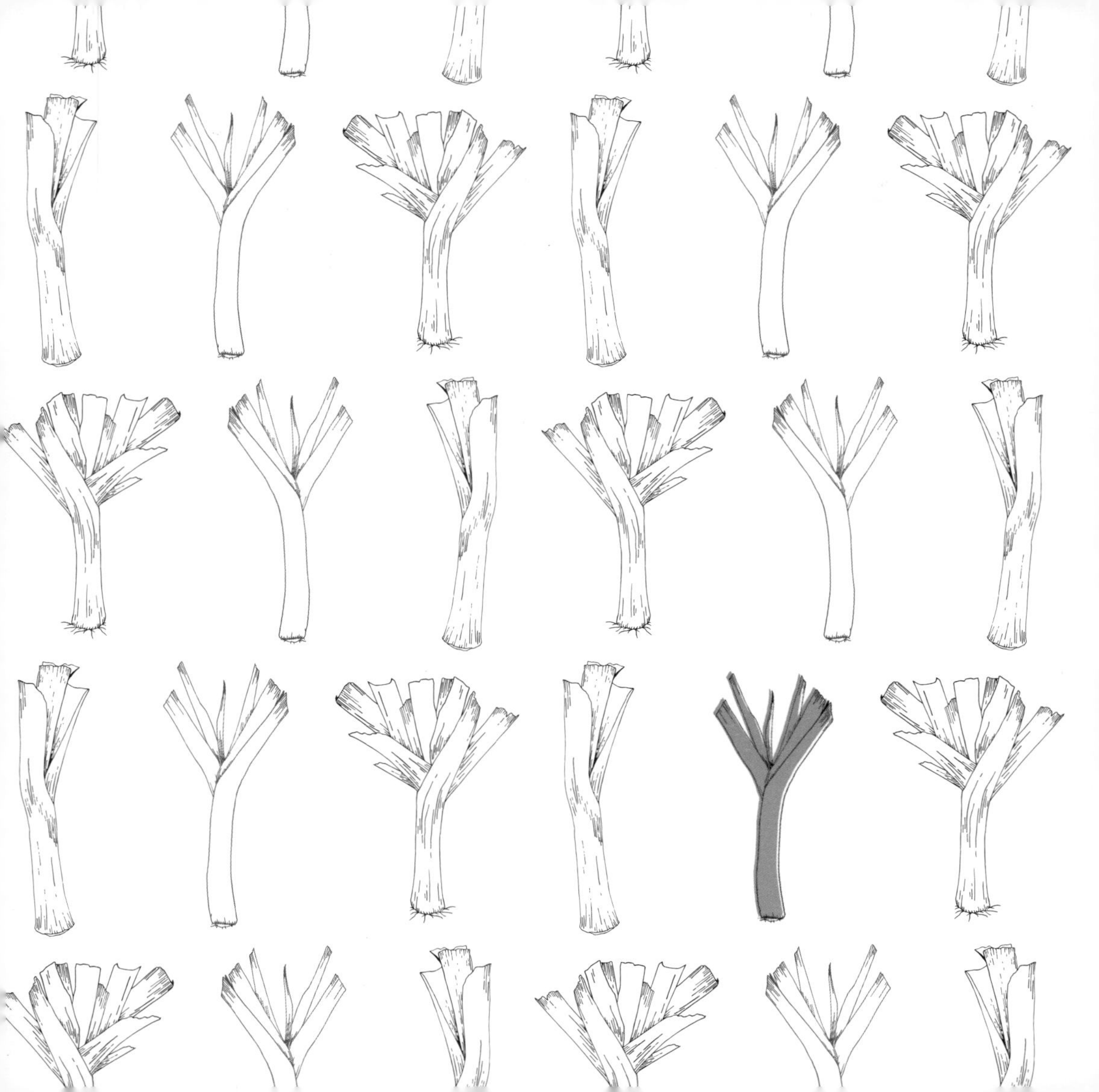

LOBSTER BISQUE

50g butter, preferably unsalted

half a leek, finely diced

½ teaspoon paprika

2 tbs tomato puree

1 tbs plain flour

300ml dry white wine

55ml dry sherry

2 tbs sage/thyme, finely chopped

225g flaked lobster meat

225g/1 227g tub Rodda's clotted cream

25g parsley, finely chopped

seasoning

1 bay leaf

Melt the butter and gently sauté the diced leek. Combine the paprika and tomato puree before adding to the pan and stirring carefully.

Add the flour, stir well before incorporating the wine and sherry in small amounts, stirring all the time. Add the sage/thyme and bay leaf and leave to simmer for 20 minutes.

Mix in the flaked lobster meat before bringing slowly to the boil. At this point, the Bisque may be liquidised to form a smooth soup. Return to a clean pan, add the clotted cream and heat through gently.

Serve with the chopped parsley sprinkled over the top.

WATERCRESS & POTATO SOUP

225g potatoes

2 bunches/bags watercress

300ml milk, warmed

seasoning

3 tbs cold milk

25g plain flour

25g butter

2 slices white bread

1 large clove garlic

Cook the potatoes in boiling water, drain them and reserve the cooking water.

Sieve the potatoes into a clean pan and add ¾ of the reserved water. Chop the watercress and add it to the potatoes, along with the warmed milk and seasoning.

Mix the cold milk with the flour until you have a smooth paste. Add this to the potatoes and watercress. Stir well, bring to the boil before adding the butter and serving.

Rub both sides of the bread with the clove of garlic, toast, cut into squares and sprinkle into the soup.

Alternatively, rub both sides of the bread with the clove of garlic, cut into small squares and lightly fry them before draining well on kitchen paper and again, sprinkling into the soup.

BREADS & SCONES

There really is nothing quite like the smell of home-baking to provide a comforting and homely feel. If you've never made any of these recipes before, give them a go – they really are very easy!

BROWN OATMEAL BREAD

1 tsp salt

1 tsp bicarbonate of soda

450g flour

50g lard

4 tbs coarse oatmeal

sour milk

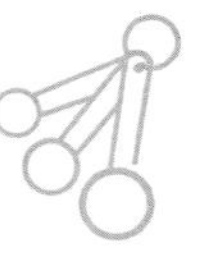

Sieve together the salt, bicarbonate of soda and flour and mix very thoroughly. Rub in the fat until it resembles fine breadcrumbs, then mix in the oatmeal.

Make a well in the middle of the mixture, add some very sour milk until a dry, spongy dough is produced – a sticky one will make the bread heavy. Turn onto a floured board, divide into two pieces and quickly pat or roll the dough into two flat cakes.

Place on a couple of floured baking trays. Score each cake lightly into four quarters with a knife and bake for 30 minutes at 400°F/200°C.

CHEESY BREAD

225g flour

3 tsp baking powder

1 tsp salt

110g finely grated Cheddar cheese

110g mashed and sieved potatoes

milk

Sieve together the flour, baking powder and salt, making sure there are no lumps remaining, particularly of the baking powder.

Gradually add the finely grated cheese and the sieved potatoes, blending the mixture quickly with the finger tips. Add enough milk to make a soft, dry dough and make into small rounds, handling as little as possible.

Place on a floured tray and bake for about 15 minutes at 400°F/200°C.

CORNISH WHITE ROLLS

350g strong plain flour

1 tsp salt

1 tsp sugar

2 level tsp dried yeast

25g butter

10ml warm water – possibly a little more/less depending on the flour

Sift the flour, salt and sugar into a bowl. Add the dried yeast and stir well. Rub in the butter.

Mix in enough water to form a smooth dough. Knead the dough for 15-20 minutes until it becomes smooth and elasticated. Place in a lightly oiled bag/bowl and leave for 1 hour to prove. 'Knock back' the dough before dividing it into 6 equal-sized pieces and shaping to the desired form.

Place on an oiled baking sheet and leave to prove for 30 minutes, before cooking in a hot oven (400°F/200°C) for 15-20 minutes.

You will know they are cooked by 'knocking' on the bottom of each roll; it should sound hollow.

FRUIT SCONES

225g flour

1 tsp cream of tartar

½ tsp bicarbonate of soda

good pinch salt

50g butter

50g mixed dried fruit*

120ml milk

Sieve together the flour, cream of tartar, bicarbonate of soda and the salt. Lightly rub in the fat, and add the mixed dried fruit. Form a well in the mixture and add sufficient milk to form a spongy, dry dough.

Knead gently for a moment, place on a floured board and lightly roll out to about 2cm thick.

Cut into rounds, arrange on a floured tray and bake at 425°F/220°C for about 10 minutes.

*Traditionally, this refers to currants, sultanas and raisins. However, there is now a huge variety of other dried fruit, including blueberries, strawberries, apricots and such like.

Why not try some of these in your fruit scones?

CHEESE SCONES

110g flour

1 tsp baking powder

pinch salt and pepper

10g butter

25g cheese

milk

Sieve together the flour, baking powder, salt and pepper. Rub in the butter. Grate and add the cheese.

Add sufficient milk to make a soft dough. Knead and shape to about 1cm thick.

Mark into quarters with a knife, brush with milk and bake for about 10 minutes at 400°F/200°C.

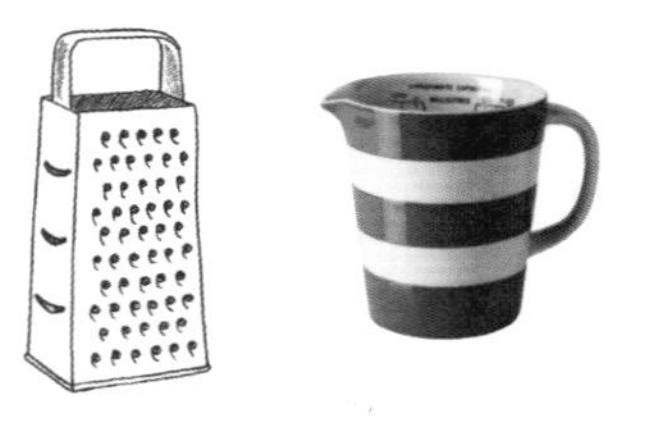

OATMEAL SCONES

50g medium oatmeal

175g flour

good pinch salt

½ tsp bicarbonate of soda

½ tsp cream of tartar

50g butter

sour milk

Carefully sieve together the flour, salt, bicarbonate of soda and the cream of tartar. Rub in the butter with the fingertips.

Make a well in the centre of the mixture and gradually add the milk to form a soft and spongy dough which 'cleans' the basin and yet is not sticky. Quickly and lightly roll out on a floured board to about 2.5cm thickness.

Cut into rounds, place on a floured baking tray and bake for about 8 minutes at 425°F/220°C.

CURRANTY BREAD

1125g white flour

2 tsps salt

50g lard

450g currants

50g candied peel

25g yeast

10g caster sugar

480ml milk

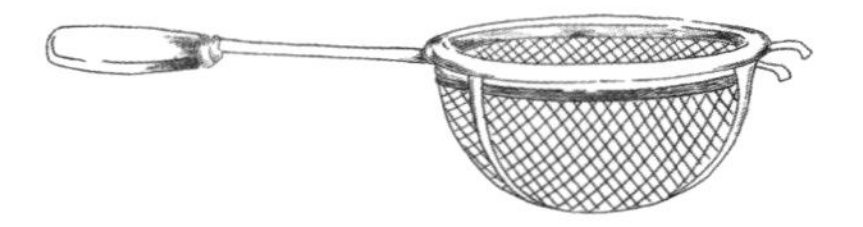

Sieve together the flour and salt. Rub in the lard until it resembles fine breadcrumbs and then add the chopped-up peel and fruit.

Cream the yeast with the sugar and mix in the milk. Pour the liquid into a well, made in the centre of the flour, cover it with a sprinkling of the flour, place a clean tea-towel over the bowl and leave in a warm place for 30 minutes.

Then carefully mix to a soft dough, knead thoroughly and leave again in a warm place until twice the size. Cut into about four pieces to half fill several greased and floured tins. Place once more in a warm spot until the dough has risen to fill the tins.

Bake for a quarter of an hour at 425°F/220°C, then a further hour at 375°F/190°C.

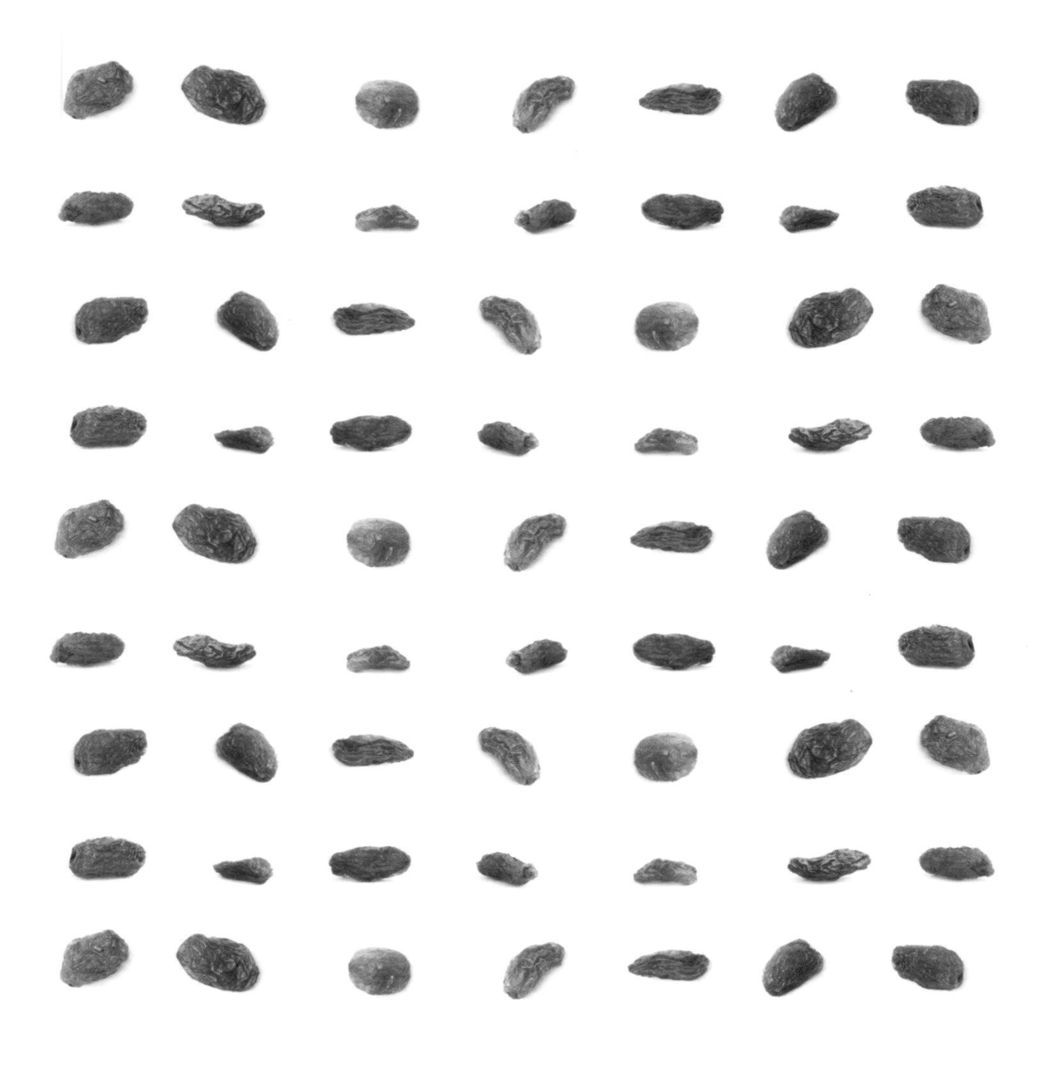

CURRANT LOAF

450g flour

1 level tsp salt

50g lard

50g butter

110g sugar

20g yeast

about 240ml milk

1 egg

110g currants

50g sultanas or candied peel

a little nutmeg

Sieve the flour and the salt together and rub in the fat. Add the sugar. Cream the yeast with a spoon until liquefied.

Warm the milk and pour on to the beaten egg. Add this to the yeast and pour the mixture on to the flour. Beat well and set aside in a warm place, covered, to rise. After about one hour mix in the fruit, candied peel and nutmeg.

Divide into two greased loaf tins and set in a warm place to 'prove', or rise, and fill the tins.

Bake for about 15 minutes at 400°F/200°C and then at about 25 minutes at 350°F/180°C.

FISH & MEAT

Cornwall has become noted for its tradition of local meat producers and butchers working together to keep food miles to the minimum. Fishmongers and butchers around the country do exactly the same, by providing quality fish and meat at fairly-traded prices. Don't be afraid to ask their advice with a recipe; they will be delighted you are taking an interest in their produce.

A CORNISH FRY-UP

6 slices streaky bacon, preferably dry cured

1 large onion

3 large potatoes

seasoning

water/stock

Fry the bacon in a deep-sided frying pan, adding the onion before the bacon is completely cooked. Fry gently for a further 3 to 5 minutes.

Add the thinly sliced potatoes. Cover with a lid and simmer until the potatoes are soft. Add seasoning and enough cold water/stock to more than cover the ingredients.

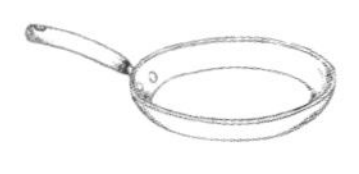

BACON & EGG PIE

1 packet shortcrust pastry

6 rashers of smoked back bacon, cooked or uncooked according to your taste

8 eggs, 1 separated into yolk and white

150ml double cream

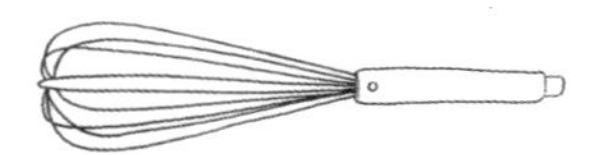

Divide the pastry into ⅓ and ⅔. Using the larger ⅔, roll out and line a fluted flan dish. Lay the bacon over the base of the flan dish.

Break 6 of the eggs over the bacon, evenly spacing each one around the dish. Mix the remaining egg and separated yolk with the double cream before pouring over the bacon and egg mixture.

Roll out the remaining ⅓ of pastry and place over the top of the pie, sealing the edges with a little egg and cream mixture. Bake at 400°F/200°C for 25 minutes until cooked.

Insert a clean knife into the centre to check for cooking; if it comes out clean, the pie is ready.

Note: Take care not to burn the pastry. If the pie looks as though it is browning too quickly, turn the heat down slightly and adjust the cooking time.

BAKED SCALLOPS

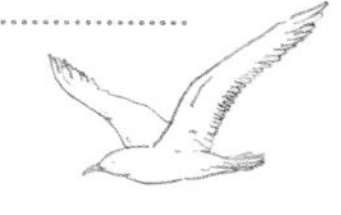

scallops

lemon Juice

golden breadcrumbs

butter

Scallops are very tasty baked in the oven. Take them out of the shells, throw half of these away and well scrub the rest. Wash the scallops, removing the dark part and the beard. Cut the edible flesh into small pieces, placing this in the remaining shells.

Sprinkle lemon juice and golden breadcrumbs over the scallops, add small pieces of butter then bake for 30 minutes at 350°F/180°C. A sheet of greaseproof paper placed over them in the oven will prevent drying out.

BEEF STROGANOFF

225g/1 227g tub Rodda's clotted cream

2 tsp dark French mustard

2 tbs sunflower oil

450g rump steak, thinly sliced

180ml red wine/beef stock

1 leek, finely diced

12 mushrooms, sliced

25g butter

½ a small cauliflower, divided into small florets

25g parsley, finely chopped

Mix the cream and French mustard together, and set aside. Heat the oil in large pan and fry off the steak. Once browned all over, add the wine, bring to the boil and leave to simmer until you are ready.

Gently fry the leeks and mushrooms in the butter until soft. Cook the cauliflower florets in boiling water until just cooked, before draining and adding to the leeks and mushrooms.

Add the beef and sauce to the vegetables, stir lightly before mixing the clotted cream and mustard, along with the parsley.

Note: Cornish beef herds continue to thrive across the county. Ask a local butcher for details of where their beef is sourced; it's perfectly possible it comes from a farm local to the village.

BETTY STOGS' DINNER

450g good quality steak

1 large sliced onion

raw potatoes cut into large pieces

2 large carrots cut into chunks

300ml Betty Stogs bitter

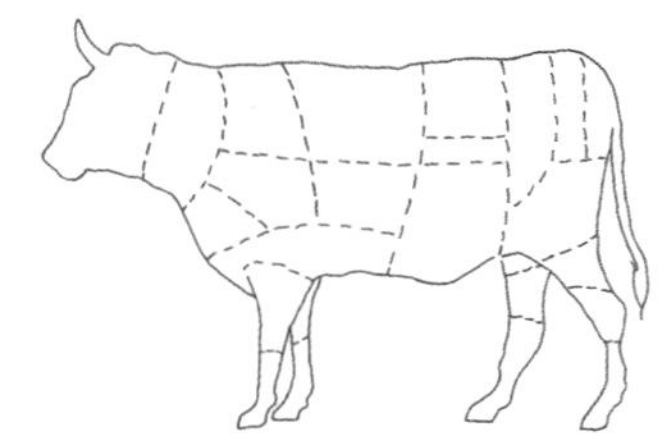

Cut the meat into strips, removing any excess fat. Dip each one in seasoned flour and roll up. Arrange rolls on the bottom of a dish and cover with sliced onions. Add the potatoes & carrots, one or two pieces of fat cut off the meat and almost cover the contents of the dish with Betty Stogs bitter. Cook in a moderate oven (325°F-400°F/170°C-200°C) for at least one hour.

Serve with Potato Cream Cake (see page 36).

CHEESY FISH PIE

450g boiled cod

25g onion, finely chopped

25g butter

25g flour

240ml fish stock

seasoning

½ tsp cayenne pepper

1 tsp mustard

Worcester sauce

vinegar

25g parsley, chopped

50g grated cheese

900g potatoes

Cover the fish with cold water, bring to the boil and simmer until tender. Drain, saving the liquid. Remove the skin and bones from the fish while still warm, and flake the flesh. Fry the onion in the butter on a low heat until soft. Add the flour, stirring, and then the stock (milk can be used as part of the quantity).

Bring to the boil, simmer until it thickens, stirring all the while. Add the salt and pepper, the dry mustard, and a few drops each of Worcester sauce and vinegar, and the parsley and cheese.

Mix in the flaked fish, turn in to a greased ovenproof dish and top with the potatoes nicely mashed and creamed. Put the dish in a moderate oven (325°F-400°F/170°C-200°C) for about 15 minutes and serve piping hot.

DRESSED CRAB

crab

chopped parsley

seasoning

white breadcrumbs

vinegar

A live crab must be plunged in deep boiling water, well salted, to kill it. Boil for about twenty minutes, drain and cool. Overcooking will harden the flesh. Remember that the claw meat is white and that in the shell brown, so if choosing a ready cooked crab keep your family's preference in mind.

Most people would select a male crab, which has large claws and a small body. Shake the crab before buying and reject it if it sounds as though it contains water.

To dress, place the crab on its back and pull off the claws. Separate the top shell from the body of the crab. Take the shell, discard the stomach bag (just below the head) and scrape out and save all the brown meat.

Take the body, discard the grey 'dead man's fingers', remove and save the white flesh. Crack the larger claws and remove all the white meat. Season the brown flesh with vinegar, salt and pepper, and chopped parsley. Mix with a few white breadcrumbs.

Take the shell, break away the underside as far as the dark line near the edge and fill the outside with brown meat. Mix together all the white meat, season as above and fill the centre of the shell with this. Garnish with parsley.

FISH CAKES

225g mashed potatoes

225g haddock, boiled

parsley, chopped

seasoning

flour

1 beaten egg

golden breadcrumbs

Mix the mashed potatoes with the cooked fish after it has been skinned, boned and flaked. Add a little chopped parsley plus the salt and pepper.

Roll into small, flat cakes on a floured board. Brush with egg, roll in the breadcrumbs and fry for about 10 minutes, turning once.

HELFORD MUSSELS IN CREAM

1 pint fresh (Helford) mussels

2 tbs thin fresh cream

240ml prepared stock (see below)

seasoning

yolk of an egg

parsley

Thoroughly scrub the mussels under running water (the shells should be closed when bought). Prepare the stock by taking half a pint of water, and adding a little salt and pepper, 1 tsp of vinegar, a pinch of mixed herbs, 1 clove and a piece each of carrot, celery and onion. Simmer until the vegetables are soft, allow to cool, and strain.

Then place the mussels in the stock and bring to the boil, gently agitating the pan. When the shells open remove the mussels, cut away the beard and lay on a dish, each resting in half the shell. Cover with a cloth or lid. Simmer the stock for five minutes, allow to cool a little and gradually add the beaten eggs and cream. Reheat gently and pour over the shellfish.

Garnish with parsley.

POTATO CREAM CAKE

450g potatoes

2 medium onions

seasoning

1 packet shortcrust pastry

150ml double cream

Peel the potatoes and onions and slice thinly. Season well. Place in a colander, cover and allow to drain for 30 minutes.

Place a pie-funnel in the centre of a round, greased baking tin. Arrange the potato and onion slices in the tin, cover with shortcrust pastry and bake for about half an hour at 420°F/215°C (check to ensure the pastry does not burn).

Pour the cream through the funnel, return to the oven for 10 minutes or so to heat through. Serve with roast meat or Betty Stogs' Dinner (see page 31).

PROPER CORNISH PASTIES

A homemade Cornish Pasty is one of the 'wonders of the west', whether it includes meat, vegetables or fish. While the filling may differ, the pastry part of a Proper Cornish Pasty always remains the same.

A PROPER CORNISH PASTY

MAKES 2

450g shortcrust pastry

110g chuck or stewing steak

175g potatoes

50g swede

1 small onion, chopped

3 tbs cold water

seasoning

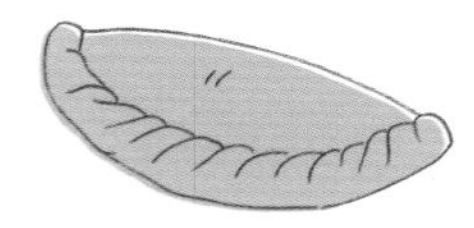

Make the pastry and roll out to about 5mm thick. Cut into rounds, using a saucer or a small plate. Cut the meat into small pieces, rejecting anything inedible such as gristle, lumps of fat, or bone. Dice the raw potato and finely chop the onion.

Mix the meat, swede, onion and potato together very thoroughly, add salt and pepper and about three tablespoonfuls of cold water. Place some of this filling on one half of each circle of pastry, damp the edges of the latter with cold water and fold the pastry over to cover the mixture.

Press the edges of the pastry together and crimp it with the fingers to seal. Make two or three ventilating slits in the 'lid', brush with beaten egg or milk if a glaze is required, and place on a baking tray.

Cook in a hot oven (450°F/230°C) until the pastry is pale brown, then reduce the heat to 350-375°F/180-190°C for about 40 minutes.

BREAKFAST PASTY

MAKES 2

450g shortcrust pastry

6 slices of streaky bacon

2 eggs hard-boiled

seasoning

2 chipolata/slim sausages

2 tbs baked beans

tomato ketchup/brown sauce to taste

Make the pastry and roll out to about 5mm thick. Cut into rounds, using a saucer or a small plate.

Take three slices of streaky bacon and one hard-boiled egg to each pasty. Rind and dice the bacon, add the egg, shelled and flaked, as well as a chipolata, 1 tablespoon of baked beans, seasoning and a lugg of tomato ketchup/brown sauce to taste.

Press the edges of the pastry together and crimp it with the fingers to seal. Make two or three ventilating slits in the 'lid', brush with beaten egg or milk if a glaze is required, and place on a baking tray.

Cook in a hot oven (450°F/230°C) until the pastry is pale brown, then reduce the heat to 350-375°F/180-190°C for about 40 minutes.

Note: To make more pasties, increase the amount of pastry and multiply the ingredients.

BACON & EGG PASTY

MAKES 2

450g shortcrust pastry

6 slices of streaky bacon

2 eggs hard-boiled

chopped parsley

seasoning

Make the pastry and roll out to about 5mm thick. Cut into rounds, using a saucer or a small plate.

Take three slices of streaky bacon and one hard-boiled egg to each pasty. Rind and dice the bacon, add the egg, shelled and flaked, as well as the chopped parsley, pepper and salt.

Press the edges of the pastry together and crimp it with the fingers to seal. Make two or three ventilating slits in the 'lid', brush with beaten egg or milk if a glaze is required, and place on a baking tray.

Cook in a hot oven (450°F/230°C) until the pastry is pale brown, then reduce the heat to 350-375°F/180-190°C for about 40 minutes.

CORNISH FLORENTINE PASTY

MAKES 2

450g shortcrust pastry

1 bunch parsley

1 bunch/bag watercress

1 bag spinach

2 eggs, beaten

seasoning

Make the pastry and roll out to about 5mm thick. Cut into rounds, using a saucer or a small plate.

Wash and spin the parsley, watercress and spinach. Place in a pan with a lid and wilt over a gentle heat. Remove from the heat and place into a colander before leaving to stand for 25 minutes, preferably with a heavy plate on top to help the water drain through.

Place the vegetables on rounds of pastry, crimp each pasty except at one point and pour into this a small amount of beaten egg. Seal the pasties and bake as usual.

MY VEGETABLE PASTY

MAKES 2

450g shortcrust pastry

350g mixed vegetables - try aubergine, courgette, peppers, leeks & cauliflower

25g of cheese, if desired

seasoning

egg

Make the pastry and roll out to about 5mm thick. Cut into rounds, using a saucer or a small plate. Dice the mixed vegetables of your choice. Aubergine, courgette, peppers, leeks, cauliflower in fact, just about anything works well here.

Thoroughly mix the vegetables, seasoning and about three tablespoons of cold water. Place some of this filling on one half of each circle of pastry, damp the edges of the latter with cold water and fold the pastry over to cover the mixture.

Press the edges of the pastry together and crimp it with the fingers to seal. Make two or three ventilating slits in the 'lid', brush with beaten egg or milk if a glaze is required, and place on a baking tray.

Cook in a hot oven (450°F/230°C) until the pastry is pale brown, then reduce the heat to 350-375°F/180-190°C for about 40 minutes.

Note: You may wish to include 1oz of cheese with your mixture; Cornish Blue cheese works particularly well but whatever you have in the fridge will be sure to be delicious! Cook as before.

HERB PASTY

MAKES 2

450g shortcrust pastry

1 bag parsley

1 bunch watercress

1 bag spinach

2 leeks or shallots

4 rashers of bacon

egg

Make the pastry and roll out to about 5mm thick. Cut into rounds, using a saucer or a small plate.

Chop and scald a quantity of well washed parsley, watercress and spinach. Cut up finely some shallots or leeks and the rashers of bacon. Place the vegetables and bacon on rounds of pastry, crimp each pasty except at one point and pour into this a small amount of beaten egg.

Make two or three ventilating slits in the 'lid', brush with beaten egg or milk if a glaze is required, and place on a baking tray.

Cook in a hot oven (450°F/230°C) until the pastry is pale brown, then reduce the heat to 350-375°F/180-190°C for about 40 minutes.

SWEET POTATO & PARSNIP PASTY

MAKES 2

450g shortcrust pastry

225g swede, diced

110g parsnip, diced

225g sweet potato, diced

seasoning

egg

Make the pastry and roll out to about 5mm thick. Cut into rounds, using a saucer or a small plate. Dice the swede, parsnip and sweet potato into small pieces.

Mix together the vegetables, add seasoning and about three tablespoons of cold water. Place some of this filling on one half of each circle of pastry, damp the edges of the latter with cold water and fold the pastry over to cover the mixture.

Press the edges of the pastry together and crimp it with the fingers to seal. Make two or three ventilating slits in the 'lid', brush with beaten egg or milk if a glaze is required, and place on a baking tray.

Cook in a hot oven (450°F/230°C) until the pastry is pale brown, then reduce the heat to 350-375°F/180-190°C for about 40 minutes.

NEWLYN PASTY

MAKES 2

450g shortcrust pastry

175g fish fillet

seasoning

1 bunch of parsley, chopped

2 eggs, hard-boiled (if desired)

Make the pastry and roll out to about 5mm thick. Cut into rounds, using a saucer or a small plate.

Simmer a portion of fish fillet – haddock, cod or whatever you like – in a small amount of milk and seasoning until cooked. Remove the fish from the liquid and leave to cool before gently flaking. Mix with the chopped parsley and egg and divide up onto the pastry rounds. You may wish to add, cheese and/or vegetables to taste. Damp the edges of the rounds with cold water and fold the pastry over to cover the mixture.

Press the edges of the pastry together and crimp it with the fingers to seal. Make two or three ventilating slits in the 'lid', brush with beaten egg or milk if a glaze is required, and place on a baking tray.

Cook in a hot oven (450°F/230°C) until the pastry is pale brown, then reduce the heat to 350-375°F/180-190°C for about 40 minutes.

MANACCAN PRIMROSE PASTY

MAKES 2

450g shortcrust pastry/sugar pastry

4 large Manaccan (cooking) apples, diced

4 tsp brown sugar

50g of raisins/sultana/other fruit

seasoning

Manaccan Primroses are a type of traditional Cornish cooking apple found on the Lizard. While any cooking apple will be fine for the recipe, the Manaccan Primroses have a taste all of their own!

Mix all the ingredients together and sprinkle with a very small amount of water to moisten. Divide the ingredients up onto the pastry rounds. Damp the edges of the rounds with cold water and fold the pastry over to cover the mixture.

Press the edges of the pastry together and crimp it with the fingers to seal. Make two or three ventilating slits in the 'lid', brush with beaten egg or milk if a glaze is required, and place on a baking tray.

Cook in a hot oven (450°F/230°C) until the pastry is pale brown, then reduce the heat to 350-375°F/180-190°C for about 40 minutes.

A CORNISH CREAM TEA

Afternoon tea is one of Cornwall's greatest pleasures. Scones - or splits if you prefer - with homemade jam and clotted cream. To make your cream tea especially Cornish, remember it's the cream that's the most important part - on the top of everything else!

CORNISH CLOTTED CREAM

full cream milk

Choose a wide, shallow earthenware pan. Strain very fresh milk into this and leave to stand, overnight if summertime or for twenty-four hours in cold weather. Then slowly, and without simmering, raise the temperature of the milk over a low heat until a solid ring starts to form around the edge.

Without shaking the pan, very carefully remove it from the heat and leave overnight, or a little longer, in a cool place.

The thick crust of cream can then be skimmed off the surface with a large spoon or a spatula.

CORNISH CREAM SYLLABUB

2 lemons

4 tbs brandy

4 tbs sherry

175g caster sugar

600ml Cornish double cream

flakey chocolate bar, for serving

Grate and juice the lemons, leaving the peel to seep in the juice for several hours. After this, add the brandy, sherry and sugar stirring until dissolved.

Whip the cream. Slowly add the lemon mixture to the cream, a little at a time to stop it from curdling, until a soft, smooth curd is produced. Spoon into pretty glasses and chill before serving with a sprinkling of flaked chocolate over the top.

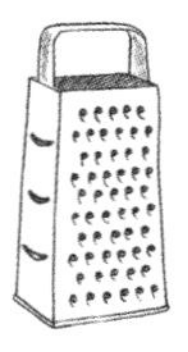

CORNISH SPLITS

240ml milk

1 tsp caster sugar

25g yeast

450g white flour

1 tsp salt

50g lard

Warm the milk. Cream the sugar and yeast together and mix with the milk. Sieve together the flour and salt, rub in the lard and add all this to the liquid mixture to form a soft dough. Knead thoroughly, leave in a warm place to rise, knead again and then shape into round buns.

Put on a lightly floured baking tray, leave to prove once more, then bake for about 15 minutes at 400°F/200°C.

Splits may be served hot or cold and to make them Cornish, always spread the jam first, followed by the cream on top.

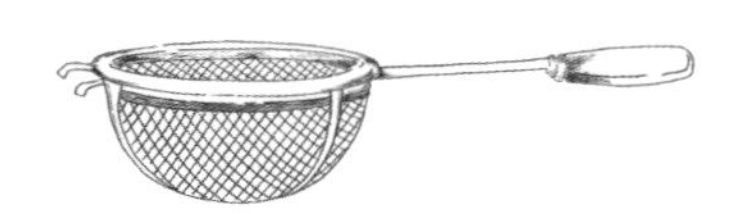

CREAMED APPLE

6 apples

3 tbs caster sugar, sieved

225g/1 227g tub Rodda's Cornish clotted cream

1 tsp lemon juice

cinnamon, for serving

Bake the apples until soft before spooning out the insides and passing through a sieve. Beat in the caster sugar before folding in the cream and lemon juice.

Spoon into pretty glasses and chill before serving with a sprinkling of cinnamon over the top.

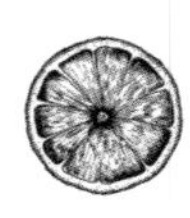

MINI RASPBERRY MERINGUES

450g/1 453g tub Rodda's clotted cream

8 mini meringue nests

8 raspberries per meringue nest

fresh mint, washed and spun in a salad spinner

Place one tablespoon of clotted cream into each meringue nest. Cover with raspberries and place a mint leaf on each one. You may wish to sprinkle icing sugar over the top of each one just before serving.

Note: these nests work equally well with blueberries, blackcurrants, strawberries, blackberries in fact, just about any fruit!

CHAPEL PORTH HEDGEHOG ICE CREAMS

ice cream of your choice, usually vanilla but it could be any flavour

ice cream cones, one per person

1 small tub Rodda's clotted cream

chocolate sprinkles and/or finely chopped nuts

Place a scoop of ice cream on top of the cone and cover with clotted cream. Roll the ice cream in either the chocolate sprinkles or finely chopped nuts, or even both. When you have a good covering, start licking!

Another variation of this is the Smiley Face; for this, substitute the nuts for jelly beans and use to make eyes, nose and mouth. Chocolate sprinkles make the hair. Enjoy!

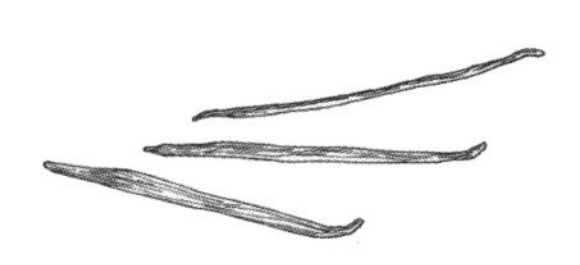

HOMEMADE TEACAKES

110g butter

225g self raising flour

110g currants

50g sugar

25g candied peel

½ tsp mixed spice

240ml milk

egg, beaten

Rub the butter into the flour, then add the currants, sugar, peel and mixed spice. Add sufficient milk to make into a soft dough.

Roll out to 1cm thickness and cut to shape with a round cutter. Brush with beaten egg to glaze and bake at about 350°F/180°C for 10 to 15 minutes.

These are nice split and spread with butter.

CAKES & BAKES

A proper Cornish tea really is one of the delights of being on holiday - the food, the cream and having the time to watch the world go by as you eat. Try eating Launceston Cake with a side of Cornish clotted cream - you'll be amazed at the difference it makes.

CORNISH FAIRINGS

- 225g flour
- ½ tsp salt
- 2 tsp mixed spice
- 3 tsp ground ginger
- 1 tsp cinnamon
- 2 tsp baking powder
- 2 tsp bicarbonate of soda
- 110g butter
- 110g sugar
- 4 tbsp golden syrup

Sieve together the flour, salt, spices, baking powder and bicarbonate of soda. Mix in the butter and add the sugar. Spoon the syrup into a cup, stand in shallow water in a pan and heat gently until runny.

Pour the liquid syrup on to the other ingredients and work in thoroughly. Flour the hands and roll the mixture into small balls. Place on a greased baking tray, well-spaced out.

Bake at 400°F/200°C for around 8 minutes, moving the biscuits from the top to the bottom shelf of the oven the moment they begin to brown.

ST AUSTELL TRIBUTE CAKE

225g butter

350g sugar

240ml Tribute ale

2 eggs

675g currants

450g flour

1 tsp bicarbonate of soda

½ tsp mixed spice

Melt the butter over a very gentle heat and when melted, add the sugar, Tribute ale and well beaten eggs. Mix the fruit in the flour and add this.

Lastly add the bicarbonate of soda and the mixed spice and stir thoroughly for several minutes.

Divide into equal parts and bake in two tins at about 350°F/180°C for at least two hours.

MADE IN CORNWALL CHOCOLATE CAKE

175g caster sugar

175g butter, at room temperature

175g self raising flour

2 tsp baking powder

2 tbs milk

3 eggs

225g Made in Cornwall chocolate in a flavour of your choice, broken into small pieces

Mix together the sugar, butter, flour, baking powder, milk and eggs until you have a smooth mixture. Spoon into a large tray-bake tin. Scatter the chocolate over the top of the cake mixture before baking in a moderate oven (325°F-400°F/170°C-200°C) for 20 minutes or until cooked.

Serve warm with clotted cream as a pudding or as part of an afternoon tea.

MANACCAN APPLE CAKE

175g caster sugar

175g butter, at room temperature

175g self raising flour

2 tsp baking powder

2 tbs milk

3 eggs

225g Manaccan apples, or other cooking apples, peeled and sliced

brown sugar for sprinkling

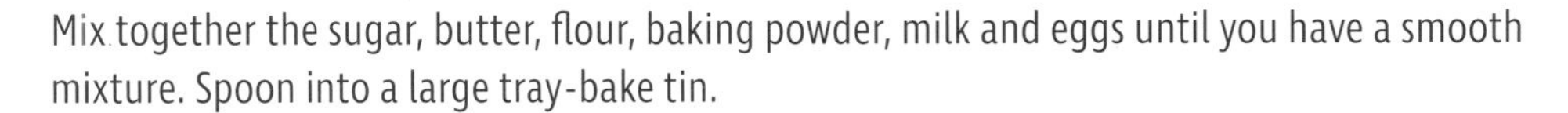

Mix together the sugar, butter, flour, baking powder, milk and eggs until you have a smooth mixture. Spoon into a large tray-bake tin.

Randomly place the apples over the cake, pushing well down into the mixture. Sprinkle the sugar over the top.

Bake in a moderate oven (325°F-400°F/170°C-200°C) for 20 minutes or until cooked.

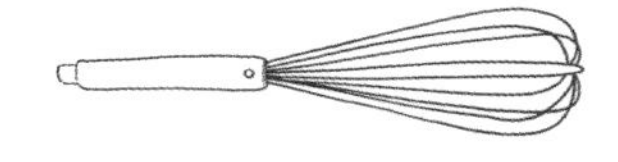

LAUNCESTON CAKE

175g sugar

175g butter

½ tbs black treacle

1 tbs golden syrup

3 eggs

225g flour

50g ground almonds

450g currants

50g lemon peel

Cream the sugar and fat, add the treacle, syrup and then the eggs one at a time, beating each one in thoroughly before adding the next.

Lastly, mix together the flour, almonds, currants and lemon peel, and fold them carefully into the mixture.

Bake at 350°F/180°C for about 90 minutes.

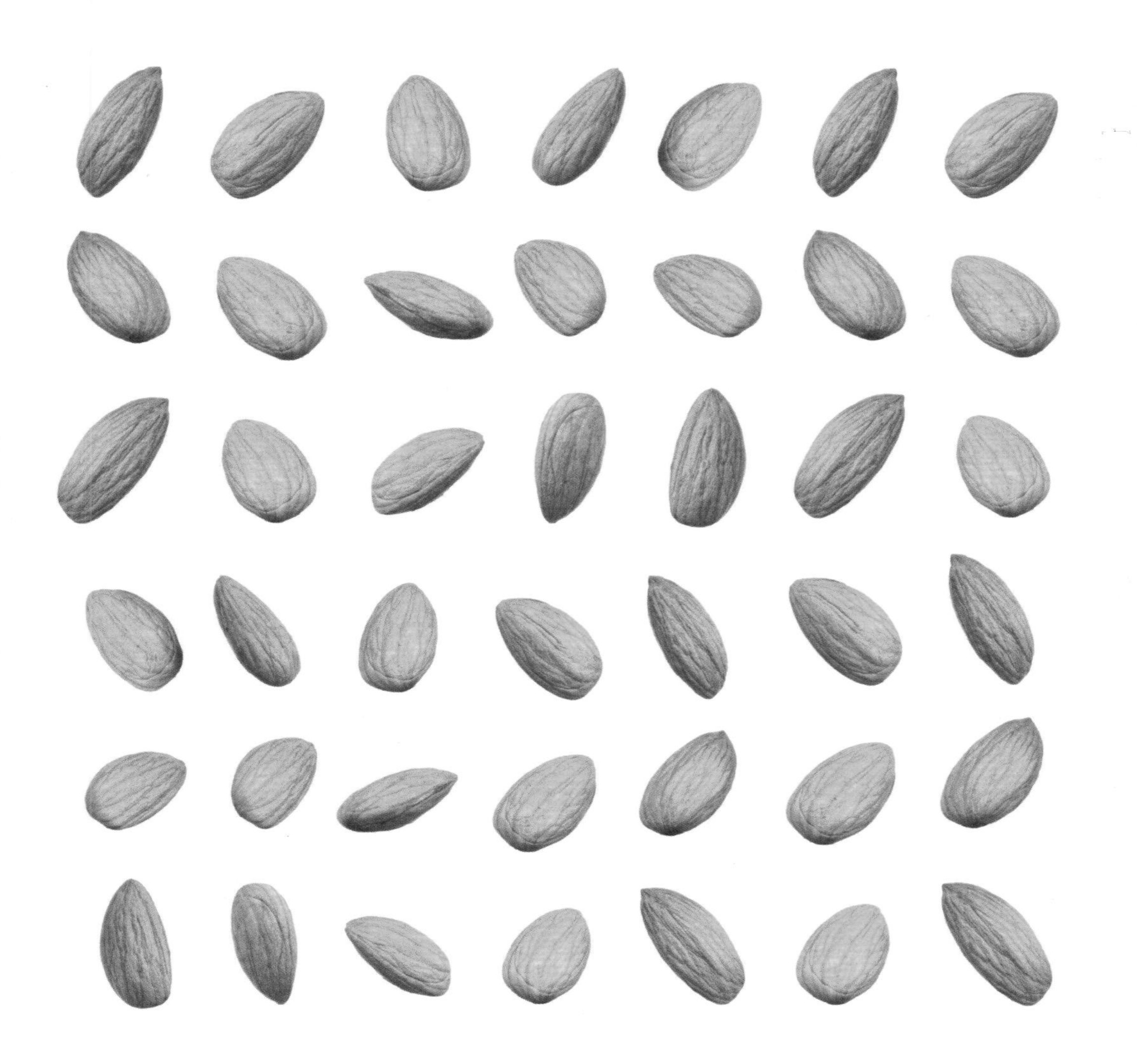

MY CORNISH FRUIT LOAF

150g/200g dried fruit (currants and sultanas)

175g demerara sugar

300ml tea

275g self raising flour

1 beaten egg

Soak the fruit and sugar in 300ml of warm tea overnight. The next day add the flour and beaten egg. Bake in a lined oblong cake tin for about 30 minutes at 375°F/190°C.

Best eaten the next day, sliced and buttered. It is also very good toasted and buttered.

SAFFRON CAKE

2g of saffron

450g butter

900g flour

pinch of seasalt

110g sugar

50g candied peel, finely chopped

450g currants, finely chopped

a little warm milk

25g yeast

Cut up the saffron and soak overnight by adding a little boiling water, which it will flavour and stain a bright orange. Rub the butter into the flour, add the salt, sugar, finely chopped peel and currants.

Warm a little milk and pour it over the yeast and one teaspoonful of sugar in a basin. When the yeast rises, pour it into a well in the centre of the flour, and when the yeast rises through this and breaks it, mix the whole by hand into a dough, adding milk as needed, as well as the saffron water. Leave in a warm place to rise for a little while.

Bake in a cake tin for about one hour at 350°F/180°C.

SEEDY CAKE

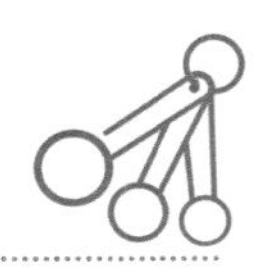

110g butter

110g sugar

2 eggs

175g flour

½ tsp baking powder

salt

1 tsp caraway seeds

milk

Cream the butter and sugar together, then add and beat in the eggs one at a time. Sieve together the flour, baking powder and the salt, and add the caraway seeds.

Fold into the creamed butter, sugar and eggs, adding enough milk to make the mixture drop off a spoon.

Bake for about 60 minutes at 400°F/200°C.

ST AGNES' GINGERBREAD

450g white flour
½ tsp salt
2 tsp baking powder
½ tsp bicarbonate of soda
1½ tsp ground ginger
10g lemon peel, finely grated
175g butter
175g treacle
175g golden syrup
225g brown sugar
1 egg
240ml milk, warmed

Sieve the flour, salt, baking powder, bicarbonate of soda and ginger together. Add the finely grated lemon peel. Put the butter, treacle and sugar into a pan and melt gently over a low heat. Beat the egg and add this to the warmed milk.

Mix all the ingredients together very thoroughly and divide into tiny balls rolled round in the palms.

Space widely on a greased baking tray and cook for about 10 minutes at 400°F/200°C.

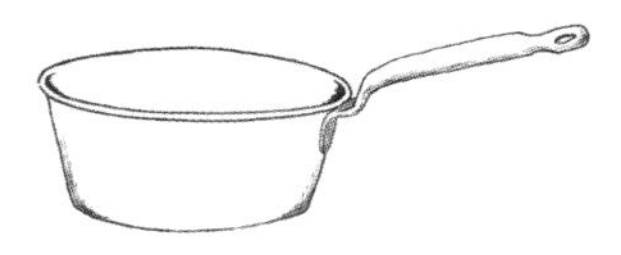

HEAVY CAKE

110g lard/butter

450g flour

½ tsp salt

175g sugar

350g currants

about 120ml milk

110g butter

Rub the lard/butter into the flour and add the salt, sugar and fruit. Mix to a soft dough with the milk. Turn on to a floured board and roll out to a long strip about 15cm wide.

Distribute half the butter in small pieces over the top two-thirds of the pastry. Fold the bottom third without lard/butter upwards and then the top third down over it.

Give the pastry a half turn so that the folds are at the sides. Roll out again into a thin strip and spread the rest of the butter as before, repeating the folding in the same way.

Roll out finally into a square about 1cm thick. Score the top into a lattice pattern, brush with egg and bake for about thirty minutes at 400°F/200°C.

SWEETS & TREATS

Making something sweet to eat can turn a dull, drizzly day into something quite special. Invite a friend to join you – these recipes should very definitely be shared.

CORNISH CLOTTED CREAM FUDGE

250g caster sugar

110g golden syrup

225g/1 227g tub Rodda's clotted cream

Grease a square cake tin.

Mix together all the ingredients in a heavy-based pan. Heat gently until the sugar has dissolved and the ingredients look glossy and smooth. Bring to a rolling boil for 3 minutes or until the mixture reaches 240°F/116°C.

Remove from the heat, beating all the time, until the mixture becomes thick, creamy and loses its sheen. Pour into the tin and leave to set. A little before it is completely set, you may wish to mark out a grid for cutting into squares later.

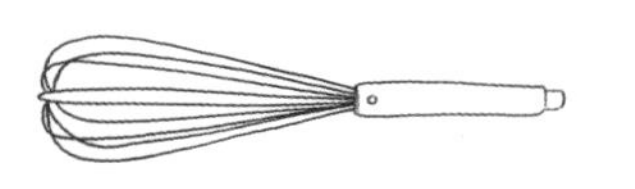

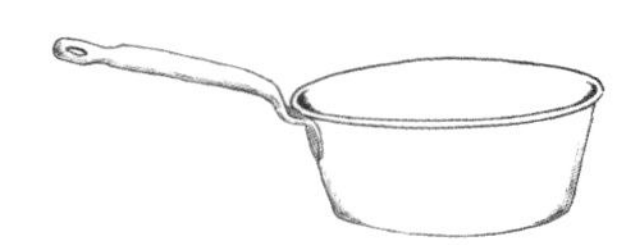

WHEAL ROSE SALTED CARAMEL TOFFEE

75g golden syrup

75g black treacle

175g soft brown sugar

75g butter

¼ tsp cream of tartar

1 tsp Cornish salt flakes

Make me on a dry day! A damp or humid atmosphere may affect the toffee by increasing the amount of moisture it absorbs.

Place all the ingredients in a heavy-based pan and melt to combine, stirring occasionally, over a gentle heat. Bring the mixture to a rolling boil until the temperature reaches 185°F/85°C.

Pour the mixture into a lined and greased square cake tin. For even pieces of toffee, wait until the mixture is almost set before scoring lines along the top. For a more casual appearance, wait until firmly set before removing from the tin and breaking with a rolling pin.

WHEAL KITTY FUDGE

110g butter

450g granulated sugar

400g condensed milk

150ml milk

1 tbs golden syrup

¼ tsp vanilla essence

Melt the butter and stir in the sugar. Place the condensed milk, ordinary milk, golden syrup and vanilla essence into a jug before adding to the butter and stirring until the sugar dissolves.

Bring the mixture to a steady boil, stirring continuously. After about 20 minutes the sugar thermometer should show 'soft ball' stage (116 degrees).

Remove from the heat and stir (a mixer is easiest) until the fudge starts to change from a glossy to a matte finish. Do NOT be tempted to overbeat the fudge as it will become dry.

Immediately pour the mixture into your prepared tin and use a sheet of parchment to level the top. Leave the fudge to cool before it cutting into squares.

Note: If you overbeat the fudge do not despair! Melt it again slowly over a gentle heat with 360ml of water. Stir continuously before bringing the mixture up to 116 degrees and repeat as above, being careful not to overheat. Some recipes advise beating for 20 to 25 minutes, although this recipe usually requires a beating time of only 5 minutes.

Cocktails make everywhere an exciting treat, and Cornwall extra-specially so! Cornish Mead makes a good base for your cocktail making, containing as it does a sweetness to which a sharp contrast may be added.

CORNISH MEAD

4.5l water

1.3kg honey

50g root ginger

25g yeast

Boil the water for half an hour before use, then add the honey and boil for one hour more, skimming off any froth that rises to the surface.

Cut up the ginger and bruise it (Jamaica ginger is best). Place it in a muslin bag and add to the liquid. When almost cold add the yeast. Bottle, and when it has finished working, cork tightly.

Mead may be drunk hot or cold. The longer it is kept the better the flavour.

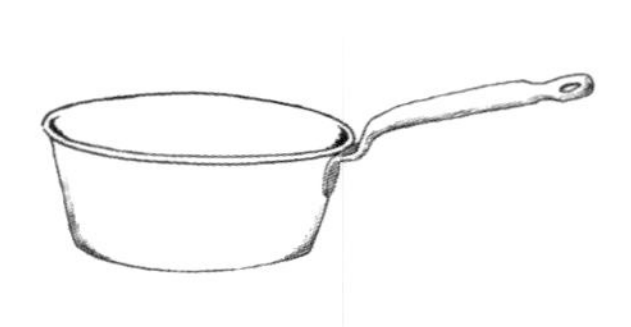

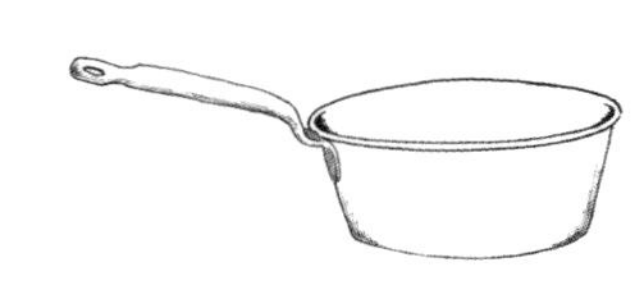

ELDERFLOWER WINE

4 lemons

4 oranges

112g root ginger

960ml elderflowers

3.6kg brown sugar

9l water

50g wine yeast

Thinly slice the fruit into a large earthenware or plastic container, add the lightly-bruised ginger, the elderflowers and the sugar.

Boil the water and pour on to these ingredients. Allow to cool slightly and add the yeast. Leave to stand for several days, stirring twice a day.

Strain carefully through clean muslin. Bottle and cork.

After approximately six weeks, store the bottles on their sides in a cool dark cupboard.

SLOE WINE

2l sloes

1.8kg granulated sugar

2l water

Ensure only ripe, black sloes are used, but make certain none of them are shrivelled. Pour boiling water over the sloes in a large container and leave to soak for a week in a warm place.

Stir the mixture twice a day. Add the sugar gradually and stir thoroughly until dissolved.

Bottle and cork loosely, then tighten the corks when the working is finished. Keep at least six months before use.

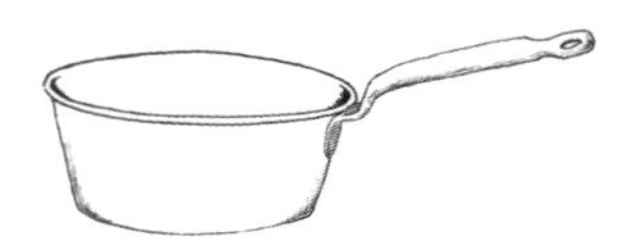

ST AGNES' MULLED WINE

1 bottle Shiraz

150ml orange juice

1 sprig fresh rosemary

50g sugar

2 parcels of mulled wine spices & herbs

Named after the locally famous mulled wine served in the Parish Church on St Agnes' Christmas Late Night Shopping evening.

Combine the ingredients in a pan over a gentle heat until the sugar has dissolved. Increase the heat until a mild simmer appears around the edges of the wine. Leave to simmer for 8 minutes before turning the heat down. Serve when ready.

Note: this recipe may be multiplied although three bottles of wine is usually the optimum number in any one preparation.

WINTER SPRUCE CRUSH

450g sugar

2 tsp tartaric acid

4.5l water

1 tsp ground ginger

half a lemon – juiced & with the rind chopped into small pieces

1 parcel of spices and herbs

Dissolve the sugar in 480ml of the boiling water. Add the other ingredients, including the juice of the lemon and the chopped rind.

Dilute to one gallon with the rest of the water (cold).

FOR THE ADVENTUROUS...

Star Gazey Pie is famously baked on 23rd December to remember how Mousehole was saved from famine by Mowzer the cat and a local fisherman, Tom Bawcock. The annual display of Christmas lights, coupled with the thousands of visitors to the village every year, make this an intriguing and unique dish.

STAR GAZEY PIE

1 pack shortcrust or flaky pastry of your choice

4 eggs, hard-boiled

4 rashers streaky bacon

1 leek

butter for frying

8 pilchards, gutted, boned and carefully washed

1 lemon

chopped parsley

seasalt

Divide the pastry into ⅓ and ⅔, rolling out the ⅔ and lining the base and sides of a deep-sided pie dish. Boil the eggs for 6 minutes (depending on the size) before peeling and cutting them in half. Chop the bacon and leek into small slices before lightly frying in butter. Arrange the bacon and leek over the base of the dish. Scatter parsley over this.

Now, either arrange the pilchards around the edge of the dish, each with their head sticking over the side. Tuck the eggs in between each fish and squeeze the lemon juice over. Roll out the pastry and cover the body of the fish crimping the pastry neatly at the edges;

OR arrange the eggs over the leek, bacon & parlsey mixture, cover the whole lot with the remaining pastry and crimp at the edges. Carefully cut a large cross in the centre of the pastry and peel it back before pushing each pilchard's tail into the dish and underneath the pastry, leaving the head sticking out. Fold back the pastry and tuck around the fish. Brush with a mixture of milk and egg for a shiny glaze.

Cook at 400°F/200°C for around 20 minutes or until the fish is cooked and the pastry golden.

NOTES